Hail, Reader!

I am Dormeo, a dormouse, gladiator, berry nibbler, and your guide to ancient Rome. My ancestors have lived on the Palatine Hill since the time of the twins Romulus and Remus. In fact, one of my relatives was actually eaten by the she-wolf who adopted those wild twins! My family has witnessed the rise and fall of Rome. We have also had the terrifying honor of being a favorite food of the Romans — there have been many times when the only thing between me and a Roman's digestive juices was my gladiator's helmet, so I won't be taking that off, even for you! However, I will tell you everything you need to know about the ups and downs of life in Rome. Just keep me supplied with berries or I might . . . [yawn] . . . be forced . . . [yawn] . . . to hibernate . . . [large yawn] . . . before you have finished reading.

Semper vale et salve,

Dormeo Augustus

P.S. *Semper vale et salve* means "best wishes" in Latin which is the language of all good Romans.

P.P.S. This letter is written on a scrap of scroll I rescued from the city of Rome as it fell about my twitching whiskers!

P.P.P.S. Snore . . .

Southwest Branch

NO LONGER PROPERTY
SEATTLE PUBLIC LIBRARY

9010 35th Ave SW
Seattle, WA 98126-3821

FOR IGGY
In theobroma
cacao fidemus!

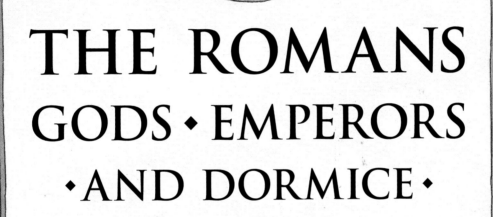

THE ROMANS
GODS · EMPERORS
· AND DORMICE ·

written and illustrated by
MARCIA WILLIAMS

CANDLEWICK PRESS

FROM MUDDLE TO HUMANKIND!

Follow your guide. That's me, Dormeo!

The Romans borrowed many myths.

They also borrowed gods and spirits — mostly from the Greeks!

Res vera means "fact" in Latin.

Am I up or down?

Should I be awake . . .

or asleep?

In the beginning, the world was a great big muddle.

I need to know where I am!

Then a god decided to sort the whole mess out.

You there and you there!

He divided night from day and the land from the sea and sky.

One for Moon. One for Sun.

He also created a myriad of creatures and plants.

It's fine for you, up in the clouds, but I need some friends down here.

Well, you create them; it's my rest day!

Most of his relatives were really impressed. Only Prometheus was disappointed. He was lonely and wanted a few friends.

RES VERA
The Romans believed that humans are special because they stand up, with their eyes turned toward the stars. Other creatures hang their heads toward the ground.

So Prometheus took some damp clay and squished it and squashed it until he had created hundreds of little versions of himself, which he called humans.

Men and women quickly multiplied and made their home on the earth.

Although they looked just like little gods, they didn't have the gods' amazing powers.

Luckily, many of the gods and goddesses stayed on earth to care for humankind, but the most powerful gods lived in a huge palace on top of Mount Olympus.

Me, asleep? Never!

Prometheus was the cousin of Jupiter, king of the gods.

He was a craftsman and made all sorts of things (not just humans).

He lived on earth, but he was allowed to visit Mount Olympus . . . sometimes!

RES VERA
The gods punished Prometheus for stealing fire by chaining him to a rock.
Each day a vulture tore out his liver — and each night his liver grew again!

THE GODS AND GODDESSES . . .

So I'll have to be careful!

The people Prometheus created had to keep the twelve most powerful gods on Mount Olympus happy—otherwise the gods wouldn't keep them safe. They built temples in the gods' honor and chose priests and priestesses to organize their festivals and sacrifices. They ignored the gods at their peril, for the Roman gods were quick to anger and slow to forgive!

You're the one for me!

What's he up to?

JUPITER

The god of the sky, thunder, and lightning, and the king of all the gods, Jupiter helped people stay on the path of honor and duty. If he was upset, he would throw lightning bolts! Jupiter's wife, Juno, was very fiery—even Jupiter was scared of her. Luckily, he could change himself into an animal and hide from her.

JUNO

Juno was the queen of the gods, goddess of women and marriage. Juno was youthful, lively, strong, and jealous. She had an amazing bodyguard, Argus, who had a hundred eyes. Juno was Jupiter's sister as well as his wife, and she had two children, Mars and Vulcan.

You have to watch Juno. She's very warlike.

Coo!

Grumpy!

Woof!

MINERVA

Minerva was the goddess of wisdom and Jupiter's favorite daughter. She was born from his brain and was both beautiful and powerful. Juno hated her.

APOLLO

Another of Jupiter's children, Apollo was the god of the sun, music, healing, and prophecy. He was warmhearted and popular. Wherever he went, sunshine and music followed in his path.

DIANA

The twin sister of Apollo and goddess of the moon and hunting. Diana could talk to animals and make them obey her. Unlike Apollo, Diana was cold-hearted and loved only her dogs.

They say Minerva invented numbers and musical instruments.

Jupiter sent Mercury to deliver dreams to earthlings.

MERCURY

Jupiter's youngest son and a firm favorite with the Romans, Mercury was born with a twinkle in his eye and grew up to be clever and very speedy, so Jupiter made him the messenger to the gods. All the gods and goddesses trusted Mercury with their secrets!

RES VERA
As Rome expanded, the number of gods also grew. The Romans adopted new gods from the places they invaded.

OF MOUNT OLYMPUS

The Roman people loved their gods, goddesses, and spirits. They saw them in flowers, in streams, on door latches, even under their beds. There were special gods to protect people in the countryside, with public shrines to honor them, and each home had a shrine in honor of the household gods. Vesta, the goddess of fire, was also worshipped in every home.

Where's the action, babe?

MARS

The most important god after Jupiter, Mars was the god of war, nature, spring, and cattle. He was the son of Juno and a magic flower! Mars was a handsome, vain troublemaker who loved battles and bloodshed. The other gods tried to avoid him and his sidekick, Discordia, who was the spirit of disagreement.

Wouldn't you like to know?

VENUS

The goddess of love, vegetation, and beauty, Venus was dear to every Roman's heart. She was born from sea foam and rose up from the sea on a shell as a fully grown woman. Venus married Vulcan, but she hated being tied to him. She was always on the lookout, among both gods and mortals, for a more exciting love.

Venus, my dove!

VULCAN

Vulcan was the god of fire and forge. If he stoked his furnaces too hard, volcanoes erupted! He adored Venus, even though she mistreated him. He was the son of Jupiter and Juno and was born with a limp.

VESTA

The goddess of the hearth and home, Vesta was sister to Jupiter and Juno. Unlike her siblings, she was kind and watched over women, who honored her by throwing cakes into their fires.

Where is my daughter?

CERES

The goddess of the harvest, Ceres was Jupiter's third sister. If she was upset, then crops failed and people starved. When her daughter, Proserpina, vanished, the fields became deserts until she was found.

The god of the sea and fresh water, Neptune was the brother of Jupiter and Dis, the god of the underworld. He was powerful, moody and very good-looking, with green hair and blue eyes. He only visited Mount Olympus occasionally, as he preferred to ride his horses through the waves.

Be good to the gods, and they'll be good to you.

Mars would love to mash my bones!

Venus, the bringer of joy to gods and dormice.

I'm in hiding — Neptune likes fish, but he hates dormice!

RES VERA
The goddess of Rome was Roma.
Her image appeared on early Roman coins.

THE BIRTH OF ROMULUS AND REMUS

Long before Rome was even thought of, the great god Mars traveled from Mount Olympus, through the gate of clouds that led to earth, to marry Princess Silvia of Alba Longa, in the country now called Italy.

Silvia's father, King Numitor, had lost his crown to Amulius, his wicked brother.

Amulius was furious when Mars and Princess Silvia had twin sons.

He feared that the twins would try to reclaim their grandfather's throne.

So he took the twins and threw them into the Tiber River.

RES VERA
Some say that after the birth of the twins, Amulius buried Silvia alive.
She was rescued by the river god Tiberinus, who later married her.

RES VERA
Roman historian Titus Livius wrote about the discovery of Romulus and Remus:
"A shepherd found the she-wolf feeding the twins and licking their faces."

KING NUMITOR'S CROWN

One day, Romulus and Remus got into such a serious fight
that the local judge was called.

He looked at the twins with interest—
they seemed so familiar.

The twins told him the strange story
of their childhood.

Suddenly, the judge, who had once been King Numitor, realized
that Romulus and Remus must be his lost grandchildren.

RES VERA
It is believed that a woodpecker helped the she-wolf feed the twins.
The wolf and the woodpecker are both sacred animals of Mars.

Numitor told Romulus and Remus how their uncle Amulius had taken his kingdom and imprisoned their mother.

In a fury, Romulus and Remus tracked down Amulius and killed him.

Then they rescued their mother from the dank, dark prison.

The kingdom of Alba Longa rejoiced to see the family reunited and good King Numitor's crown restored!

RES VERA
The kingdom of Alba Longa was in a part of Italy called Latium. The Latin tribe had settled there, as the land was close to the Tiber River and very fertile.

THE FOUNDING OF ROME

The year is now 753 BCE.

After a time, Romulus and Remus decided to build their own kingdom on the seven hills of their childhood.

Remus built a city on the Aventine Hill.

Romulus built a city on the Palatine Hill.

One day, Remus mocked Romulus's city wall.

Romulus was so angry that he killed Remus and took his city!

RES VERA
Early Rome was more like a group of small farms than a city.

THE SEVEN KINGS OF ROME

REX I — ROMULUS

Much of what we know about early Rome and its first seven kings comes from ancient stories. The Romans believed that Romulus and the six kings who followed him helped to create a structure for Roman society that lasted for hundreds of years.

Romulus exhausted the Romans with his battles.

Numa always listened to the gods — clever man!

The stories about these kings were written long after they'd died.

Not even a dormouse can tell what's true and what's false!

REX II

NUMA POMPILIUS r. 715–673 BCE
After Romulus vanished, the Senate appointed a Sabine, Numa Pompilius, as Rome's new king. Numa was wise and peaceful, and he turned the wild barbarians of Romulus's reign into peaceful Roman citizens. They learned to respect other people's boundaries and to take pride in their crafts and trades. Numa died of old age.

REX III

TULLIUS HOSTILIUS r. 673–642 BCE
Tullius Hostilius was the third king of Rome. He never took advice from the gods and loved a good battle. He even destroyed Alba Longa, once ruled by King Numitor. When a terrible plague spread through Rome, Tullius became ill and turned to the gods for help. He was too late—Jupiter fired off a bolt of lightning, which hit Tullius's house and reduced it and Tullius to ashes!

REX IV

ANCUS MARCIUS r. 642–616 BCE
Ancus Marcius was the fourth king of Rome. He was the grandson of Numa Pompilius, and he honored the gods and wanted peace. King Ancus built the first bridge across the Tiber River and extended Rome's territory to the sea, founding the port of Ostia. He built a salt works there, which helped the Romans to preserve their food and make it tastier!

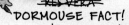

~~RES VERA~~
DORMOUSE FACT!
I, Dormeo, am the greatest Roman historian ever known to man or dormouse!

The Rome that Romulus lived in was a collection of simple villages.
As the population grew, these were united into a city, and the
Forum Romanum, Rome's first city center, was built.
As each King captured more land, Rome's influence spread.

ROMULUS
d. 715 BCE

REX V

TARQUINIUS PRISCUS r. 616–579 BCE
Tarquinius Priscus was the fifth King of
Rome. He was the guardian of King Ancus's
teenage sons and stole the throne from
them. He built the first sewer, some great
roads, and the Circus Maximus, for chariot
racing and boxing. In the end, King Ancus's
sons had him assassinated, but they still
didn't get the throne, as Tarquinius had
already appointed his successor.

REX VI

SERVIUS TULLIUS r. 579–535 BCE
Servius Tullius was the sixth King of Rome.
He was born a slave but was adopted by
Tarquinius. He was caring and popular.
Under his rule, Rome grew to cover all
seven hills, and the first Roman coins
and census were introduced. Servius's
reign ended when he was dragged from
his throne and murdered by Tarquinius
Priscus's grandson, Tarquinius Superbus.

REX VII

TARQUINIUS SUPERBUS
r. 535–509 BCE
Tarquinius Superbus was the
seventh and last King of Rome.
The Roman people never forgave
him for the murder of Servius Tullius.

He ruled by fear and killed
or persecuted anyone who
disagreed with him, and his son
Sextus was no better. The pair behaved
so abominably that the Roman people finally
rebelled and drove Tarquinius into exile.

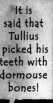
It is
said that
Tullius
picked his
teeth with
dormouse
bones!

The
Romans
believed
the gods
chose
Tarquinius
Priscus
as king.

My mom
said Servius
was really
the son
of an
Etruscan
princess.

Before
coinage,
Romans
swapped
goods
instead
of using
money.

RES VERA
Servius Tullius organized the Romans into classes: patricians were landowners, equites were businessmen,
plebeians were poor citizens, and slaves and people from outside Rome were noncitizens.

THE REPUBLIC OF ROME

Shh, nunc dormio.

After the Romans rid themselves of King Tarquinius Superbus in 509 BCE, Rome became a republic—it was ruled by the people through the Senate.

Really, the senators ruled.

A lictor carried the consul's fasces.

Instead of a king, two consuls were chosen to help the Senate.

Most men were given the vote, but women and slaves weren't.

The new republic continued to capture more land.

The fasces was a bundle of sticks and an ax.

Every time Rome won a battle, it grew stronger and richer.

Eventually, the Romans ruled the whole of Italy, and Rome became its capital city.

The consul could use the fasces to beat or kill you.

RES VERA
A diet of dormice, grain, and honey kept the Roman army fit.

THE GRUESOME GAULS

Shh, I'm still asleep.

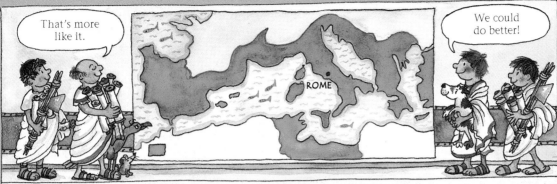

That's more like it.

We could do better!

ROME

The ambitious Romans fought on, conquering lands around the Mediterranean Sea.

Crazy barbarians!

Get out of our land!

As Rome's power spread, the barbarians fought back.

It's those Gauls again!

Arrgghhh!

Around 390 BCE, the Gauls from northern Europe invaded Rome.

Run! The city is burning!

The Roman people fled to the Capitol Hill.

Honk!

Honk, honk!

Honk!

The Gauls attacked the Capitol under the cover of darkness.
The Romans were asleep, but luckily the sacred geese of Juno were keeping guard!
Their honking alerted the sleeping Romans and so saved the city.

Some fought for Rome, others for wealth and glory.

If you weren't a Roman, you were a barbarian!

The Gauls fought in the nude.

But they wore amulets to protect them!

Buzz, buzz!

~~RES VERA~~
DORMOUSE FACT!
I think it was the sight of the Gauls'
naked bodies that started the geese honking!

JULIUS CAESAR

As the Roman Republic grew, it became harder and more expensive to govern. Some senators tried hard to help the people, while others cared only for their own wealth and power.

The Roman people were taxed heavily.

Paid workers were replaced with unpaid slaves.

Many citizens became poor and hungry.

Julius Caesar, a powerful Roman general, promised to banish hunger from the streets of Rome.

The people were delighted. Caesar became a Roman dictator, but many senators feared that he wanted to be king.

RES VERA
On the way to Rhodes to study oratory, Caesar was captured by pirates. He managed to escape and later had the pirates executed.

Watch out for army generals!

The senators grew fatter, the people thinner.

I've lost many relatives to hungry Romans.

Caesar was a great orator.

THE ROMAN EMPIRE

March 15, 44 BCE
THE IDES OF MARCH

They stabbed him 23 times!

Who will look after Rome now?

Finally, a group of senators, hoping to save the republic from Caesar's growing power and ambition, assassinated him!

Corruption.

Dirty water.

No jobs.

High prices.

Civil wars.

High taxes.

Hunger.

Without a strong leader, Rome fell into further chaos.

We will make Rome GREAT again.

Good!

Hail, Octavian!

In 27 BCE, Octavian, Caesar's adopted son, took control.

I'll be the boss, but we'll work together.

Hail, Emperor Augustus.

He kept the senators but called himself Emperor Augustus.

Friends, Romans!

We'll work hand in hand.

He's one of us.

Hail, Augustus!

He worked hard, and the Roman people liked him.

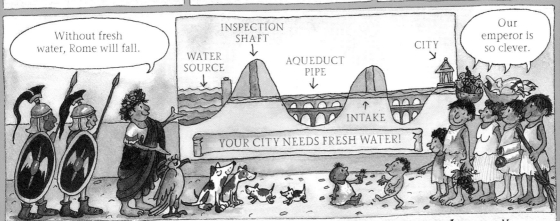

Without fresh water, Rome will fall.

INSPECTION SHAFT

WATER SOURCE

AQUEDUCT PIPE

CITY

INTAKE

YOUR CITY NEEDS FRESH WATER!

Our emperor is so clever.

The Roman Republic was over, but Emperor Augustus brought peace and prosperity to the vast Roman Empire. He created jobs, cared for the poor, reduced the size of the army, encouraged the arts, and built aqueducts to carry fresh water to the city.

Poor me!

The Senate was closed down.

Better a dormouse than a plebeian.

The plebeians liked to be heard.

Augustus means "noble." Call me Dormeo Augustus!

RES VERA
Caesar left his beautiful gardens by the Tiber River
to the Roman people.

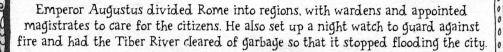

CITIZENS OF THE EMPIRE

Emperor Augustus divided Rome into regions, with wardens and appointed magistrates to care for the citizens. He also set up a night watch to guard against fire and had the Tiber River cleared of garbage so that it stopped flooding the city.

SENATORS

Senators came from wealthy families. Under Augustus, they still issued laws, but the laws had to be approved by him.

MAGISTRATES

Magistrates were also from the wealthy class. They were in charge of keeping law and order and collecting taxes.

LANDOWNERS

A landowner might have an estate outside Rome, which would be run by slaves who farmed food to be sold in the city.

SOLDIERS

A young man from a wealthy family might join the army before going into politics. Legionaries had to sign up for 25 years!

Honor the gods, citizens.

Come on, you'll make a lovely sacrifice.

Oink!

Call yourself an orator!

Baa!

He did!

I just can't believe it.

I am not paying that—it's cracked.

Tighten up that law.

More taxes?

He's so clever.

Yes, Mother.

THE FORUM was where everything happened — public speaking, banking, trading, trials, triumphal marches, festivals, shopping, and gossiping! The Basilica, a public building, was at one end and a temple at the other.

He should have cleared the cats out, too.

Gladiatorial fights and chariot races also took place in the forum.

A daily visit to the forum was a Roman must!

Wait till you see my new helmet!

We lost our home to a Roman road!

RES VERA
Absolutely everyone, from powerful senators to poor slaves, met and mingled in the forum.

Emperor Augustus continued to consult the Senate, but he was head of state, religion, and the armed forces. However, life for the citizens of Rome improved so much that most people were happy to live in an empire instead of a republic.

The crests helped the officers stand out in battle.

Fires were a huge hazard in Rome.

Dormice do not take baths.

Slaves and freedmen couldn't be Roman citizens.

CRAFTSMEN

Craft skills were passed from father to son. Rome needed many craftsmen including smiths, potters, carpenters, bakers, and sculptors.

SHOPKEEPERS

Some craftsmen made and sold their goods in the same shop. There were also lots of food shops and cafés, serving cooked food.

SLAVES

Slaves worked in mines, on buildings, in private houses, on estates, or for the government. Others worked as teachers, doctors, or librarians.

FREEDMEN

A lucky slave might buy or be given his or her freedom. Many freed slaves became craftsmen, bankers, merchants, or government clerks.

THE BATHS were an important part of Roman life. Some had hot and cold pools, toilets, saunas, cafés, exercise rooms, hairdressers, reading rooms, slave attendants, jugglers, philosophers, poets, musicians, gymnasts, and jesters!

RES VERA
Some baths could hold more than a thousand people.

Family life was important to the Romans. The dad was head of the family. If he was rich (a patrician or landowner), he would have a large house and many slaves. After breakfast, he might pray with his family at their shrine. Then he would walk to the forum to do a little trading or visit the Senate.

PATER

My family are all *nobiles*.

Many *nobiles* have a *domus* and a country villa.

All families honored the gods.

They also consulted priests and fortune-tellers.

Fortune-tellers looked for signs in the weather and animal guts.

Tiles away!

Look imperial!

Happy to help, Cousin!

Snore!

Mine!

Roar!

Pssst!

Service!

Food, slave!

Cor!

Thief!

DOMUS— CAVE CANEM

Hail!

Wakey, wakey!

Cheer up!

The patrician father would also meet with his poorer relatives and former slaves, to see how they could be helped. After lunch, he might have a siesta followed by a visit to the baths. In the evening, friends might come for a dinner served by slaves, with other slaves playing music and dancing.

WOMEN  **OF ROME**

During the republic, wealthy women did little but care for the household, but during the days of the empire, many men were away fighting, which gave women more freedom. They still attended to their households, but, encouraged by Emperor Augustus's powerful wife, Livia, they began to demand more independence and better education.

EMPRESS  **LIVIA**

Go, girls, go!

RES VERA
The Roman Senate banned the eating of dormice in 115 BCE—
but that didn't stop people from gobbling them up!

PLEBIAN FAMILY LIFE

Dormice are NOT plebeians.

MATER

Even under Emperor Augustus, life was tough for the plebeians. If they weren't jobless and homeless, they lived in cramped rooms. Their buildings' top stories were often built of wood, which was unsafe and a fire risk. During the summer, the heat was stifling and the streets stank of rotting garbage and public toilets.

Plebeian families worked all day without rest.

Dormice sleep all day without rest!

Some plebeians joined the army.

Note the ex-slave's special freedman hat.

A plebeian would rise with the sun and go to bed when it got dark. Breakfast was likely to be a slice of bread and some olives. Then the whole family, including the youngest children, would go to work. As slaves did most of the manual work, plebeians worked as craftsmen or shopkeepers or in food stalls.

SLAVES OF ROME

FREEDMAN OF ROME

Some enslaved people were born into slavery, while others were prisoners of war. There were slaves who were treated cruelly by their masters, but many others became trusted members of the household. If a slave child was lucky, he or she might even be adopted into the family.

RES VERA
Roman houses could be crowded — sons lived with their parents even after they'd got married and had children!

THE CHILDREN OF ROME

WE ARE THE FU

S · P · Q · R ·

A Roman father was the *paterfamilias* (head of the family).

He prepared his children for adulthood.

My father was eaten.

That's why Uncle Dormeo adopted me.

In the early days of ancient Rome, children had a tough time. Every newborn was handed to its father, who would decide the baby's fate. If the baby was weak, deformed, or a second girl, the father might decide not to keep it. The poor infant would be left to die or sold to a slave trader.

RES VERA
Roman families often had lots of children, as so many died either at birth or during early childhood.

...TURE OF ROME!

S · P · Q · R

Roman families often adopted children.

Infans means "little child" in Latin.

Children were usually quite strictly brought up.

But most Romans were kind to their children!

The Roman father's word was law. A child who upset his father risked being beaten, sold as a slave, or even killed! However, as the Roman Empire grew, children became more important. The boys were needed for the army, and the girls were needed to have more boys!

RES VERA
Many public buildings were inscribed with "SPQR." It stands for "Senatus Populusque Romanus," which means "the Senate and People of Rome."

A PATRICIAN CHILD'S DAY

Roman children born into a patrician family were very lucky.
They were well fed and had nice homes, as well as slaves to care for them.
Their mother or father taught them their family duties, and
most children started school at the age of about six.

PATRICIANS

MARCUS ET TULLIA

The rooster crows, Master.

Good morning, goddess Vesta.

More honey, slave.

Hurry. You're late for school.

Dad says I can come too.

What's this—a girl?

Yes, Tutor.

OK, but lose the dog!

Your brains are in your backside.

The sun is high; school is over.

Hurrah!

Siesta, then a makeup lesson.

Yes, Mater.

Siesta, then the baths.

Yes, Pater.

A Roman is strong in mind and body.

Yes, Pater.

A pretty face is a help.

Yes, Mater.

Off you go and play now.

Look!

Let's play barbarians!

No, dolls.

Let's race.

No, marbles.

Bedtime, Tullia.

What about Marcus?

I dine with the adults.

Not fair!

Say good night, Tullia.

Good night, Tullia.

RES VERA
At the *ludus*, pupils studied in Latin; with
the *grammaticus*, they also studied Greek.

A PLEBEIAN CHILD'S DAY

Rome was always noisy.

Plebeian children had a much rougher time and very short childhoods. They often had poor diets and cramped, unhygienic homes, so many died of infection or disease. Few plebeian children went to school because they had to start work at the age of five or six.

Wheeled traffic could enter Rome only at night.

All goods rumbled into the city after dark.

By day, beggars lined the roads.

Every nine days, there was a slave market.

RES VERA
If plebeian children were not out working by the age of six, they were probably looking after their siblings.

FESTIVALS

February: Parentalia festival, honoring ancestors

March: the feast of Mars

April: the anniversary of Rome's founding

August: the feast of Mercury

The Ancient Romans loved to celebrate. They had more than 200 festivals a year, celebrating everything from the gods to their own greatness! The nobles would pay for plays, pantomimes, dancing, games, or feasts, which often lasted several days. On March 1, buildings were hung with laurels to celebrate the Roman New Year.

RES VERA
On December 17, the feast of Saturnalia started.
Pigs were sacrificed, then served to slaves by their masters.

GLADIATORS

HELMET

ARM PROTECTOR

SWORD

SHIELD

GREAVE

He doesn't stand a chance!

PERFECT VISION

MUNCHING JAWS

ACUTE HEARING

POWERFUL ARM

RIPPING CLAWS

SPQR

Christians and criminals were thrown to the lions.

The Colosseum held over 70,000 people.

The wild animals came from across the empire.

Help!

The arena sand was changed only once a month!

When Emperor Titus opened the Colosseum in 80 CE, he ordered 100 days of games! In the mornings, the spectacles included dancers, jugglers, musicians, priests, and wild animals. In the afternoon, gladiators would fight, either with each other or with the animals. It was very grisly, but the Romans loved it!

RES VERA
Most gladiators didn't choose to fight — they were slaves and were forced to battle to the death. One famous gladiator Spartacus, escaped and led a slave rebellion against the Romans.

THE GREAT ROMAN ARMY

Centurions used a vine cane for beating their legionaries.

Legionarie bribed centurions to avoid a duty or punishment.

Legionaries were given financial rewards for victories.

Coronae, military crowns, were awarded for bravery.

LEGATUS

The legion commander and camp prefect, the *legatus* was usually a senator appointed by the emperor.

TRIBUNE

There were six tribunes in each legion. The chief tribune was a young noble waiting to join the Senate.

CENTURION

There were 59 centurions in command of each legion. They usually rose from the ranks.

BRONZE HELMET

ARMOR

JAVELIN

LEATHER AND WOOD SHIELD

ARTICULATED PLATE

APRON

LEATHER SANDALS WITH METAL STUDS

LEGIONARY

Training was tough for legionaries. They learned to march, swim, build camps, vault horses, and use a variety of weapons.

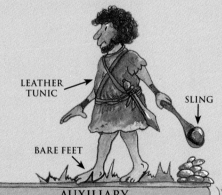

LEATHER TUNIC

SLING

BARE FEET

AUXILIARY

Auxiliaries were support soldiers. They earned less and had less training than legionaries.

Without the amazing and totally brilliant Roman army, Rome might never have ruled such a vast empire. In the early days, soldiers were part-time, but as the empire grew, a full-time army was needed. By 200 CE, the Roman army had about 300,000 career soldiers. They were skilled, well disciplined, fit, and determined! As well as learning to fight, some soldiers were trained as surveyors, engineers, or stonemasons. They supervised the construction of canals, bridges, and a vast network of roads.

RES VERA
The most prized military crown was the *corona graminea,* presented to a commander who had saved the whole legion or the entire army.

PRAETORIAN GUARD

These were the emperor's personal bodyguards. New emperors gave them huge bonuses to make them loyal. It didn't always work!

URBAN COHORTS

The urban cohorts acted as the police force in Rome. They were under the command of the city prefect.

VIGILES

A semi-military force that acted as the fire service and the night police for the fourteen districts of Rome.

Rome had three urban cohorts of 1,000 men each.

In early Rome, there were no prisons for criminals.

Criminals were fined or exiled or lost their citizenship.

Dormice were sometimes eaten with a pig-meat stuffing!

Juicy, ready cooked pig!

WAR DOG

Attack formations were sometimes made up entirely of well-trained, hungry dogs.

Oink, I'M ON FIRE!

WAR PIG

Pigs were covered in resin and set on fire. Their squealing terrified enemy elephants!

The main strength of the army were the legionaries, recruited from Roman citizens. There were about 5,000 men in a legion, divided into centuries of 80 men. Each legion also had about 5,000 auxiliaries, who were noncitizens. They served as border guards or specialist soldiers like archers and cavalrymen. The army was a good career for poor men — if they survived the 25 years they had to sign up for! On retirement, a citizen was given a small pension and plot of land, while a noncitizen was given Roman citizenship.

RES VERA
Many people think that a *vomitorium* was a room where Romans made themselves sick after eating too much, but it was actually the name for a passageway at the back of an amphitheater!

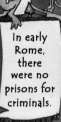

But I NEED a vomit room!

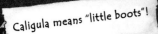
Caligula means "little boots"!

ROMAN EMPERORS—GOOD AND BAD!

Great emperor . . . and god!

GAIUS r. 37–41 CE
NICKNAMED CALIGULA

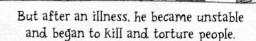

At first, Gaius was a generous and popular emperor.

But after an illness, he became unstable and began to kill and torture people.

He even tried to have his horse, Incitatus, elected consul.

After four years of this madness, the Praetorian guard murdered Gaius.

Great emperor . . . and artist!

NERO
r. 54–68 CE

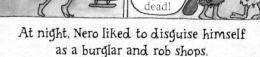

Nero started well, but then he had his mother, his wife and all his advisers murdered.

At night, Nero liked to disguise himself as a burglar and rob shops.

He did nothing for Rome. Even when it caught fire, he just continued to play his lyre.

Finally, the army rebelled. Nero committed suicide rather than risk assassination.

Rome, the little city founded by Romulus, now controlled an empire that stretched across half the known world. This made the Roman emperor the most powerful man in the world — but his job was almost impossible. Under the rule of great emperors like Augustus, the empire flourished, but not all emperors were as honorable or as clever.

RES VERA
Nero played music for hours at a time and performed in plays.
If his audience left before he had finished, they were usually killed.

Little Boots married and murdered his sister!

Incitatus had a marble stable!

Nero took part in many races and games.

Everyone let him win rather than risk his wrath!

Vespasian was a general whose legions chose him as emperor!

TITUS FLAVIUS VESPASIAN
r. 69–79 CE

After several useless emperors, Vespasian brought order to Rome.

He rebuilt parts of the city still lying destroyed by fire. He even helped clear the rubble.

Vespasian removed the corrupt from power and encouraged the good.

He was one of the few emperors who wasn't poisoned or assassinated.

Vespasian was considered a very jovial host.

He died of a nasty bout of diarrhea!

MARCUS ULPIUS TRAJAN
r. 98–117 CE

Trajan entered Rome on foot, embraced the senators, and walked among the people.

He cared for the poor and gave his own money to children in need.

He was a great emperor and general. He expanded the empire to its largest extent.

Trajan's rule brought glory to the empire, and Rome mourned his death.

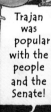

Trajan was popular with the people and the Senate!

His ashes were laid in a victory column.

Some emperors were mad, bad, and dangerous. Other emperors cared more about wealth and power than the empire and its people. Bad emperors were to be feared, but a good emperor, along with his family, would be honored and loved by the Roman people. An emperor was not thought of as a god, but the Senate could deify him (pronounce him a god) after his death.

RES VERA
The Senate prayed for new emperors to be
"More fortunate than Augustus and better than Trajan."

THE FALL OF ROME

Help! We are being attacked by Visigoths, Franks, Huns, Saxons, and Vandals!

Even strong emperors struggled to control the many miles of borders left by Trajan.

I will rule the eastern half and Maximian can rule the western, it'll be much easier.

WESTERN EMPIRE
EASTERN EMPIRE
TURKEY
ROME

In 286 CE, after years of chaos, Emperor Diocletian split the empire into two parts.

Time to get rid of that tired old symbolic eagle.

A peacock would be the perfect new symbol!

It's much nicer here than in Italy!

The Eastern Roman Empire was ruled from Constantinople, in Turkey. Eventually, it became the Byzantine Empire and thrived for a thousand years.

RES VERA
Diocletian persecuted Christians and declared that they must sacrifice to the traditional Roman gods.

THE WESTERN ROMAN EMPIRE

> Rome is crumbling.

> Alert the Senate.

> That's us!

> Snore.

In the Western Empire, the rich became richer and more interested in themselves than in Rome.

> We need work.

> And food.

> And safe homes.

The poor became poorer, and many died of disease or starvation.

I think I'll move back to the country.

> Help, I'm falling!

In 410 CE, the Visigoths attacked Rome. The Roman army was no longer a match for these fierce barbarian warriors, who ransacked the city. A series of similar attacks soon brought a sad end to the Western Roman Empire.

DANGER! ROME IS FALLING!

RES VERA
The story of Rome both begins and ends with a Romulus — the last emperor of the Western Roman Empire was named Romulus Augustus.